Teach Your Children Well

Party Princess

By Vanita Braver, MD   Illustrated by Cary Pillo

Child & Family Press   Washington, DC

Child & Family Press is an imprint of the Child Welfare League of America. The Child Welfare League of America is the nation's oldest and largest membership-based child welfare organization. We are committed to engaging people everywhere in promoting the well-being of children, youth, and their families, and protecting every child from harm. All proceeds from the sale of this book support CWLA's programs in behalf of children and families.

CHILD WELFARE LEAGUE OF AMERICA, INC.
HEADQUARTERS
440 First Street, NW, Third Floor, Washington, DC 20001-2085
E-mail: books@cwla.org

CURRENT PRINTING (last digit)
10 9 8 7 6 5 4 3 2 1

Cover and text design by James D. Melvin
Edited by Tegan A. Culler

Printed in the United States of America

ISBN-13: 978-1-58760-038-8
ISBN-10: 1-58760-038-2

Library of Congress Cataloging-in-Publication Data

Braver, Vanita.
Party princess / by Vanita Braver ; illustrated by Cary Pillo.
p. cm. -- (Teach your children well)
Summary: Six-year-old Madison learns a lesson about what true beauty is after using her mother's makeup without permission just before her birthday party.
ISBN 1-58760-038-2 (alk. paper)
[1. Beauty, Personal--Fiction. 2. Behavior--Fiction. 3. Sharing --Fiction. 4. Birthdays--Fiction. 5. Parties--Fiction.] I. Pillo, Cary,
ill. II. Title. III. Series: Braver, Vanita. Teach your children well.
PZ7.B73795Par 2005
[E]--dc22

2004029789

Dedication

To my wonderful nephews and nieces in the Braver, Kamath, and Tyerech families.

To my Bonnie Brae family with much warmth and affection.

In memory of Barbara Papetti, and to her daughter Tina Papetti Noll, who is the ultimate "Party Princess."

Acknowledgments

I would like to acknowledge my husband Joel and our three daughters, as well as Teresa and Michael Goldman, Bill Powers, Drina Simons, Georgia Schley, Karen Gruenberg, Meryl Raiffe, Jill O'Kyle, and the staff of Child & Family Press. Thank you all for your faith, hard work, and for believing in me.

Madison carefully put on her favorite dress, the fancy pink velvet one, and tied the ribbon all by herself. Then she took Wisdom the Owl down from the shelf. "Isn't my dress beautiful, Wisdom?" she asked him, dancing around her room. "I want to look extra pretty today."

Just then, the doorbell rang. Madison raced downstairs and flung open the door.

"Happy birthday!" screamed Emily, her best friend. She held a beautifully wrapped gift.

"Oooh, thanks, Emily," said Madison. "What is it?"

"I can't tell you, but it's the best present in the whole world!" replied Emily.

Madison held Wisdom up to her ear. "Wisdom is sure it is a great present, and he can't wait for the party!"

"You girls look ready to celebrate!" said Madison's mom. "Madison, you did a wonderful job of dressing yourself. You'll be the queen of the ball, and Emily will be the princess," she joked.

Suddenly, Madison remembered last Halloween when she'd dressed up as a princess. Her mom had put makeup on her face, and everyone said she looked beautiful! She had an idea.

"Would you girls like to help decorate the cake?" asked Madison's mom.

"Yes! My mom says I'm an expert cake decorator!" announced Emily.

"I want to help too," said Madison, "but first I have to finish getting ready."

Tiptoeing into her parents' bathroom, Madison quietly took out her mother's makeup case. "Maybe Mommy won't mind just this once," she thought. "After all, it is my birthday."

First she put on some bright pink lipstick. She got a little on her cheek, but she carefully wiped it off. She added blush and eyeshadow. Then Madison took out some glittery, red nail polish.

"This is perfect for a birthday princess," she thought as she brushed the polish over her pinky nail. It was so sparkly!

But suddenly, the polish dripped onto her favorite dress, leaving a sticky, glittery, red splotch on the velvet.

"Oh no!" gasped Madison. She turned to clean it up—and knocked over the whole bottle. Gooey, glittery polish spilled everywhere!

"Uh oh!" gulped Madison. "What a mess! I'd better clean this up."

Just then, Madison's mom called her name. Quickly, she tried to scrub the counter, but the nail polish wouldn't come off. Her mother called again! Madison scrubbed harder, but the polish wouldn't budge.

"Madison, what are you doing?" demanded her mother, appearing in the doorway. "I've been calling you for ten minutes. Emily and I have almost finished decorating your cake."

Then she saw the mess, and Madison's face, and the stain on her dress. "I can see you've been busy," she said with a frown. "You know better than to use my makeup without permission."

Madison started to cry. "I'm sorry, Mommy. I just wanted to look pretty for my party. But I look ugly, and I wrecked my dress, and I made such a mess!"

Her mother wiped away Madison's tears and the makeup. "Your friends will be here any minute," she said softly. "Let's find another dress and wash your face."

"What about the mess?" asked Madison.

"I don't want to think about it," replied her mom.

"Me either," said Madison.

Her mother laughed but added in a serious voice, "We'll talk about this later. Now wash your face, and I'll get your purple dress with the pink roses."

"Not that dress, Mom!" cried Madison. "It's not fancy enough!"

"It's very nice, Madison," said her mom. "And it's the best we can do right now."

When she got downstairs, Madison told Emily what happened.

"What should I do? I've ruined my party and my mom's mad," she sniffed. "And I don't like this dress!"

"I bet my present will cheer you up," said Emily, but Madison wasn't so sure.

Soon, her friends began to arrive. They played lots of party games, like musical chairs and pin the tail on the donkey, but Madison still felt sorry for herself. Afterwards, they had pizza, but Madison wasn't very hungry.

Finally, it was time for cake and presents. Madison saved Emily's gift for last. When she ripped it open, inside was the most wonderful doll she'd ever seen! Madison looked up excitedly, and saw Wisdom the Owl sitting on the table next to Emily. Then she noticed the sad look on Emily's face. She knew that Emily had wanted this doll for a long, long time.

"Wow, Emily, you were right! This is a great present!" said
Madison. "Why don't we share her?" she asked, handing the doll to
her friend.

Emily's face lit up. "Thanks, Madison!"

Madison's mom gave her a big smile. Suddenly, Madison felt
better, and she grinned back.

That night, as her mom helped her get ready for bed, Madison said, "This was the best birthday party ever!"

Madison's mom laughed. "I'm glad you had fun, honey. I'm very proud of you for sharing your doll with Emily. It shows that you are growing up. But, Madison, you are not to use my makeup without permission, okay?"

"But I just wanted to be extra pretty," explained Madison.

"I know, sweetie, but next time please ask first. Besides, you don't need to wear a fancy dress and put on makeup to be pretty. You're beautiful just the way you are, because you have such a good heart and you are so caring and giving."

Madison thought about this. "I guess sharing my doll with Emily really did make me feel better than wearing my party dress," she said.

"I thought so," said her mom, as she kissed Madison and tucked her in. "Now, good night, honey. I love you."

Madison's
mom left the room and all
was quiet. Madison closed her eyes
once and then slowly peeped them open
again. She smiled as she saw Wisdom the Owl fly
down off the shelf. He cuddled next to her.

As Madison was drifting off to sleep, Wisdom whispered into her ear, "Beauty comes from the heart. You should feel good about yourself … especially when you realize that real beauty is what's on the inside of a person, not the outside."